Riddle Rhymes

By D. J. Panec

Riddle Rhymes

Parent's Introduction

We Both Read books have been developed by reading specialists to invite you and your child to interact together as each book is being read.

In this book, you read the simple riddle on the right-hand page. (You may want to run your finger under the words as you read the riddle.) Then, before turning the page, your child tries to guess the answer. When you turn the page, the left-hand page shows the answer to the riddle with a picture and a word.

Each riddle offers two clues: a question that hints at the answer and a word that rhymes with the answer. If needed, you can help your child to think of possible answers to the hint or provide additional hints. ("Do you know what animal milk comes from?")

You can also say another word that rhymes with the answer, and ask your child to try to think of other words that rhyme or have the same ending sound. ("Log rhymes with frog. Can you think of any other words that end with the sound *og*?")

A visual hint at the answer is included in the pointing hand at the bottom of the page. (If your child doesn't need this hint, you may want to cover it with your thumb.)

If possible, try to help your child guess the correct answer before turning the page. When you turn the page, point to the word as you or your child repeats it. You might also say

What falls from louds and rhymes with train?

Rain

that this word rhymes or has the same ending sound as the word at the end of the question. ("Frog and dog rhyme. They both end with the sound *og*.")

Reading and using this book with your child will help in developing awareness of sounds in words as he begins learning to read. It will also help in developing critical-thinking skills, which are skills needed in both reading and mathematics.

After you have gone through the book once, it may be fun and helpful to go through it again with your child. Remember to praise your child's efforts and keep the interaction fun.

Try to keep these tips in mind, but don't worry about doing everything right. Simply sharing the book together will help prepare your child for reading, mathematics, and doing his or her best in school.

Riddle Rhymes

A We Both Read® Book

Use of photographs provided by Dreamstime, LLC
and iStock by Getty Images.

Published by
Treasure Bay, Inc.
P.O. Box 119
Novato, CA 94948 USA

Printed in Malaysia

Library of Congress Catalog Card Number: 2015940395

Hardcover ISBN: 978-1-60115-277-0
Paperback ISBN: 978-1-60115-278-7

We Both Read® Books
U.S. Patent No. 5,957,693

Visit us online at: www.TreasureBayBooks.com

PR 11-15

 What can you wear on your head that rhymes with *cat*?

Hat

2

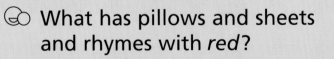 What has pillows and sheets
and rhymes with *red*?

Bed

4

 What animal barks and rhymes with *frog*?

Dog

 **What gives us milk
and rhymes with *wow*?**

Cow

 What's the opposite of day and rhymes with *white*?

Night

 What bounces high
and rhymes with *call*?

Ball

 What swims in the sea and rhymes with *squish*?

Fish

 Where can you learn
that rhymes with *pool*?

School

 What does a zebra have that rhymes with *pipes*?

Stripes

 What can you read that
rhymes with *cook*?

 Book

 What do you eat between
meals that rhymes with *stack*?

Snack

What falls from clouds
and rhymes with *train*?

Rain

What does a bunny do that rhymes with *stop*?

Hop

 What do you use to smell that rhymes with *rose*?

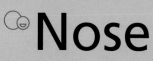 Nose

What does a puppy wag that rhymes with *pail*?

Tail

 What makes honey
and rhymes with *tree*?

Bee

What goes "quack"
and rhymes with *truck*?

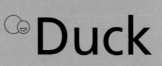

Duck

 What can you jump with
that rhymes with *soap*?

Rope

What shines all day
and rhymes with *run*?

Sun

What crawls and flies and rhymes with *tug*?

Bug

👓 What comes last and rhymes with *friend*?

The . . .

The End

To see all the We Both Read books that are available,
just go online to **www.webothread.com**

If you liked **Riddle Rhymes**, here is another We Both Read® book you are sure to enjoy!

My Car Trip

This is a perfect book to encourage even pre-readers to try reading. The rhyming patterns in the story, as well as the simple words and pictures on the child's pages, make it easy for children to participate in the reading. The simple, but delightful, story is about a young boy's trip with his parents to visit his grandfather, who owns a small general store out in the countryside.